D0459400

Food Safety:
Avoiding
Hidden Dangers

Kristin Petrie MS, RD
ABDO Publishing Company

visit us at
www.abdopublishing.com

Published by ABDO Publishing Company, 8000 West 78th Street, Edina, Minnesota 55439.
Copyright © 2012 by Abdo Consulting Group, Inc. International copyrights reserved in all
countries. No part of this book may be reproduced in any form without written permission from the
publisher. The Checkerboard Library™ is a trademark and logo of ABDO Publishing Company.

Printed in the United States of America, North Mankato, Minnesota.
062011
092011

 PRINTED ON RECYCLED PAPER

Cover Photos: Getty Images, iStockphoto
Interior Photos: AP Images pp. 22–23; courtesy CDC / Dawn Arlotta p. 24; Corbis pp. 5, 13, 25;
    Getty Images pp. 6, 10, 11, 16, 18, 27, 29; iStockphoto pp. 1, 7, 8, 14;
    Photo Researchers pp. 12, 15, 17; Photolibrary p. 19; courtesy USDA p. 20

Series Coordinator: BreAnn Rumsch
Editors: Megan M. Gunderson, BreAnn Rumsch
Art Direction: Neil Klinepier

Library of Congress Cataloging-in-Publication Data

Petrie, Kristin, 1970-
 Food safety : avoiding hidden dangers / Kristin Petrie.
    p. cm. -- (Mission: Nutrition)
 Includes index.
 ISBN 978-1-61783-085-3
 1. Food--Safety measures--Juvenile literature. I. Title.
 TX533.P48 2012
 363.19'26--dc22
                        2011012077

Contents

Food Invaders!

It is the day after a big party. You woke up during the night, feeling kind of icky. By morning, you knew you were sick. Now you're in the bathroom losing last night's dinner, your midnight snack, and everything in between.

What's wrong? Nobody else in your family is sick. However, you later learn that some other party guests feel terrible too. Now that you think about it, you all ate leftover pizza at midnight. It was cold after sitting on the table for hours. But it still tasted good.

Chances are, the pizza sat out too long and bacteria started to grow on it. Eating the pizza let the bacteria into your body, making you sick. Being sick from "bad" food is known as food-borne illness, or food poisoning.

The Centers for Disease Control (CDC) estimates a whopping 76 million food-borne illnesses occur in the United States every year. More than 300,000 of those people need to visit the hospital. And about 5,000 die.

Food is supposed to help you grow healthy and strong. It shouldn't make you sick. So keep reading. Learn about this threat and find out how to practice good food safety. Don't be the next victim of food-borne illness!

To enjoy food safely, always eat hot foods hot and cold foods cold.

Sick from Food

Most people have suffered at some point from food poisoning. It is the result of eating **contaminated** food. Nobody eats this food on purpose. Still, it happens often.

You didn't know it at the time, but the party pizza went bad during the night. It probably arrived at the party with a tiny number of bacteria on it. They may have come from someone who handled it. Or, they may have been on the pizza cutter or the cutting board.

This is not unusual. Most foods have small amounts of **germs** on them. Generally, this is not a problem because your body fights them off.

However, germs love the conditions the pizza box offered. With plenty of food and

Restaurants require workers to wash their hands. This helps keep germs from spreading to foods they handle.

Moldy food has definitely gone bad! However, foods don't have to look or smell gross to be dangerous.

Getting sick from food can make you feel like you have the flu.

a comfortable temperature, they multiplied like mad! Suddenly, the pizza was no longer safe to eat.

After your midnight snack, the bacteria traveled quietly through your stomach without making you feel sick. This is called the incubation period. It can last anywhere from a few hours to several days.

When **germs** reach your intestines, they grab on and begin to multiply. Soon, you feel sick! You may experience fever, cramping, vomiting, and more. Severe diarrhea can cause **dehydration**, which can lead to death. Babies, the elderly, and ill people are more at risk than healthy adults.

Germs can affect other parts of your body, too. Some produce a toxin that can get into your blood. This allows them to cause further harm, such as body aches or **paralysis**.

Many cases of food poisoning are caused by situations such as the leftover pizza. Tiny bacteria, viruses, or parasites may be to blame. When they cause illness, they are called pathogens.

Some plants and animals are harmful for other reasons. For example, some mushrooms and fish contain deadly toxins that are poisonous to humans. And some foods may be exposed to harmful **pesticides** or cleaning products.

Contaminated!

There are many ways in which foods become **contaminated**. Sometimes, this happens when they sit out too long or are not properly handled. Other times, it takes place at the food's source.

Like humans, animals host countless bacteria. Most of these are harmless, but others cause illness. They are carried by air, water, and food.

Bacteria can spread easily. When a cow is butchered, its intestines may be cut accidentally. Bacteria there escape and cling to other surfaces. Soon, they cover the meat and anything else it touched!

Today, most beef cattle are raised on factory farms. They live in crowded quarters, increasing the chance of spreading bacteria.

This can be a big problem. Bad meat from one cow can actually ruin a large amount of beef. This is because the meat of many cows is combined for making ground beef and other products.

In addition, equipment may not be properly cleaned after use. So, bacteria continue spreading to any other foods processed there.

Fully cooking meat is the best way to kill bacteria spread during butchering.

It is also possible for bacteria from live animals to spread to food. In a field, perhaps potatoes are **fertilized** with fresh manure. The manure carries bacteria from the animal it came from. So, the ground and the potatoes also become **contaminated**.

Later, a farmworker harvests the potatoes. What if he forgets to wash his hands afterward? Then the bacteria will pass to his food at his next meal. And after eating, they will be in his body.

In an orchard, maybe apple trees are fed with unclean water. Now the apples carry harmful pathogens. Small amounts may remain on their skins after they are picked and washed. When juice is made from the apples, it will contain those pathogens.

Other times, foods become mixed with man-made products. For example, many foods are treated with **pesticides** while they grow. Later, food coloring or preservatives are often added to foods. These make foods look better or last longer. Yet, their **side effects** are not always known. Though they are not **germs**, these types of products can still cause harm.

Be sure to practice good food safety even with natural, unprocessed foods.

Pesky Pathogens

Cross contamination is when a pathogen spreads from one surface to another. The spread of poultry juice is especially harmful.

Yikes! There are many opportunities for food to become harmful to eat. The greatest numbers of food-borne illnesses result from bacteria.

Campylobacter bacteria commonly cause food poisoning. These bacteria are naturally found in the intestines of birds. They are frequently present in raw chicken and turkey.

Food poisoning strikes after people eat undercooked poultry. It can also be caused by cross **contamination**. So, take care to use separate tools and surfaces when working with more than one food.

Salmonella bacteria are the most common cause of food poisoning in the United States. Mammals, reptiles, and birds often carry them. *Salmonella* spread to humans through undercooked foods such as poultry and eggs.

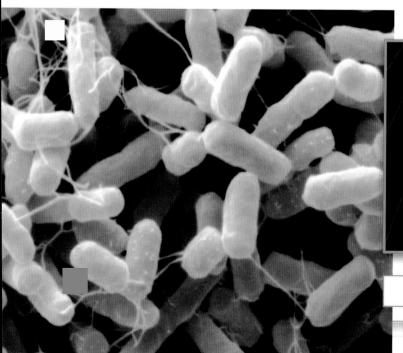

Healthy Habits

Each year, homemade ice cream results in illnesses from *Salmonella*. To make ice cream safely, use pasteurized eggs or egg substitute in your recipe.

Salmonella

> *To kill bacteria in hamburger, always cook it to 160 degrees Fahrenheit (71°C).*
> *Use a food thermometer to check for the proper temperature.*

Escherichia coli are another nasty type of pathogen. These bacteria are better known as *E. coli.* They are usually found on foods exposed to animal waste. The waste leaves tiny amounts of bacteria on meat such as beef. Touching or eating raw and undercooked meat spreads *E. coli* to humans.

Some *E. coli* bacteria naturally live in your intestines and are mostly harmless. However, certain types can cause food poisoning. *E. coli* 0157:H7 is a rare but deadly strain.

Viruses also cause food-related illnesses. A group of viruses called noroviruses is responsible for a lot of misery. They cause many cases of the food-borne illness often known as the stomach flu.

Unlike bacteria, noroviruses are not originally from animal intestines or waste. In fact, their origin is unknown. And, they spread easily from one person to another. They can also spread through food, drinks, doorknobs, and other surfaces.

We can't forget about parasites either! *Trichinella spiralis* is one that can cause food-borne illness. This tiny worm is found in the muscle tissue of some animals. It is most commonly linked to pork. It is also found in wild **game**, such as bear and fox. Humans become ill after eating the undercooked meat of these animals.

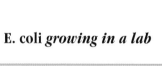

E. coli *growing in a lab*

Food Culprits

Have you noticed a trend yet? Raw and undercooked meats and poultry are the most common foods to cause sickness. **Unpasteurized** dairy products and eggs can be risky foods, too. Oysters and other raw shellfish also carry pathogens.

The risk of illness increases with mass production. Large amounts of food are combined together and then packaged. So, one package of ground beef likely contains the meat of hundreds or thousands of cows! One carton of milk may also have come from many cows. This makes it easy for just one cow to ruin a large portion of the food supply.

Washing produce before eating it can reduce surface pathogens. However, this may not completely get rid of them.

Healthy Habits

Since 1987, the FDA has required that milk be pasteurized. This process kills harmful pathogens such as *Salmonella* and *E. coli*.

Yet today, many people want the option of drinking raw milk. Supporters like that raw milk is left in its natural state. They say pasteurization destroys good bacteria and healthy nutrients. The FDA is concerned that drinking raw milk will result in more food-borne illness. So for now, its sale is limited.

Even fresh produce can cause problems. Fruits and vegetables **fertilized** with fresh manure may pick up *E. coli* or other pathogens. This also happens when produce is watered or washed with **contaminated** water.

Pathogens are usually more plentiful in the outer layers of fruits and vegetables. They are also found in the fat and skin of animals. Washing produce and trimming fat and skin from meat lowers your chances of getting sick.

Protection

Before you vow to never eat again, here is some good news. Most developed countries have laws to help keep their food supply safe. In the United States, several institutions help make the US food supply one of the safest in the world.

Inspectors and veterinarians work to make sure food is produced safely.

The first US agency to monitor food safety was the US Department of Agriculture (USDA). It was founded in 1862. One of the USDA's early tasks was to stop sick livestock from being imported. Today, it also sets quality standards and develops farming practices.

The Food Safety and Inspection Service (FSIS) is part of the USDA. This group's goal is to prevent harmful products from entering the food supply. It sends experts to meat and production plants. Others monitor imported food. The FSIS also **recalls** bad meat, poultry, and eggs.

The Food and Drug Administration (FDA) is part of the US Department of Health and Human Services (HHS). It recalls unsafe foods other than those handled by the FSIS. In addition, it checks food and health product labels for complete and correct information.

State health agencies also protect your food. When food-borne illness strikes, state and federal groups work together. They track the source and work to prevent future **outbreaks**.

The CDC aids local and state health offices. This helps them protect you and your community from future food-borne illnesses. As part of the HHS, the CDC investigates outbreaks of food poisoning on a national level. It also oversees the prevention and control efforts put in place to avoid future problems.

Canada has similar government groups. Health Canada oversees the country's public health. Its many areas of responsibility include research and educating the public about food safety and other topics. Health Canada also writes the policies and standards for the nation's food supply.

The Canadian Food Inspection Agency (CFIA) makes sure Health Canada's food standards and safety requirements are met. The CFIA also inspects foods and related products.

Like the FDA, the CFIA monitors food labeling. It also educates individuals to better protect themselves against food-related illness.

In 2011, the United States passed the Food Safety Modernization Act. It gives the FDA more power to enforce food safety.

Four Safety Steps

Washing with soap and warm water is your number one protection against food poisoning.

Here's more good news. You can protect yourself from food-borne illness with a little knowledge and practice. Try these four easy steps!

The first step is clean. Preparing food with clean hands, tools, and surfaces is your first defense. Wash your hands before and after handling food. Be especially thorough after using the bathroom or touching pets.

Separate is the second step. This means preventing cross **contamination**. Keep raw eggs, meat, poultry, seafood, and their juices away from each other and other foods. This step applies from grocery cart to kitchen.

Cold does not completely stop bacteria from growing. So be sure to eat leftovers within three to four days.

The third step is cook. Most pathogens can't stand up to temperatures of 160 degrees Fahrenheit (71°C) or higher. The minimum temperature for cooked poultry is 165 degrees Fahrenheit (74°C). Steaks are safe when heated to at least 145 degrees Fahrenheit (63°C). A food thermometer will help you know when your food is ready to eat.

Step four is chill. After you destroy **germs** with heat, keep them from coming back! Bacteria and other pathogens don't like cold. So, store leftover food at 40 degrees Fahrenheit (4°C) or lower. This slows their growth.

When in Doubt

You're feeling better, and it's time for breakfast! So you grab the milk for your cereal. Just before pouring, you notice the expiration date. The carton is stamped with yesterday's date. Now what?

Food producers voluntarily mark foods with dates. This helps consumers use products while they are at their best. However, the words used in this system can be confusing.

Some foods are stamped with a "sell by" date. It tells stores how long to display a food item. After that date, the food's quality starts to drop. However, it may not be spoiled or even near spoiling at that point.

What does this mean for you? If you want your food to taste its best, buy and use it by the "sell by" date! The same applies to foods marked with "best by" and "best if used before" dates. Still, dates on food don't always apply. For example, foods frozen promptly after purchase are safe well beyond these dates.

The USDA, FSIS, and FDA each provide guidelines about food dating, quality, and safety. You can sign up to receive their e-mail updates. When time doesn't permit extra research, a single rule will keep you safe. Just remember, "When in doubt, throw it out!"

Now you know how to keep yourself and your food safe! Use your new knowledge to avoid future cases of food-borne illness.

When you are not sure about the safety of a food, do not eat it.
It's better to throw it out than to risk getting sick!

A Healthier You

After learning about food safety, you may feel you've lost your appetite. Yet, you also know there are many ways to reduce your chances of getting sick. Apply these tips from the *Let's Move!* program to keep your diet healthy, safe, and fresh!

GET COOKING! Making a meal can be fun. And, you might enjoy eating foods you helped prepare. Before making and after eating your meal, just remember to apply the four safety steps.

IMAGINE THE POSSIBILITIES! Think leftovers are boring? Use your imagination to turn last night's meal into a new one tonight. This is also a great way to use your leftovers within a safe time frame. Check out the menu plans online at *Let's Move!* for some fresh, yummy ideas.

Let's Move!

For more information, check out *Let's Move!* online at **www.letsmove.gov**.

Let's Move! is a campaign started by First Lady Michelle Obama to raise a healthier generation of kids and combat childhood obesity. This movement works to provide schools, families, and communities with the tools to help kids be more active, eat better, and live healthfully.

The *Let's Move!* Web site provides information about the movement. It includes recipes as well as helpful tips on nutrition and physical activity. And, there are action tools to promote healthier foods in your local schools or start a *Let's Move!* Meetup.

PLAN AHEAD! Think about what meals and snacks you may want to eat during the week. Let your parent or guardian know so he or she can shop for the right amounts of each food. Buying a week's worth of groceries and eating them within that time reduces waste. It also helps you avoid spoiled foods.

Glossary

contaminate - to make unfit for use by adding something harmful or unpleasant. Contamination is the process of contaminating.

dehydration - the loss or removal of water. When lost or used water is not replaced, a person becomes dehydrated.

fertilize - to make fertile. Something that is fertile is capable of growing or developing.

game - wild animals hunted for food or sport.

germ - a tiny organism that causes disease.

outbreak - a sudden increase in the occurrence of illness, especially after eating the same food.

paralysis - the loss of motion or feeling in a part of the body.

pesticide (PEHS-tuh-side) - a substance used to destroy pests.

recall - to publicly call for the return of a product that may be harmful or unfit for use.

side effect - an often harmful and unwanted effect that occurs along with the basic desired effect.

unpasteurized (uhn-PAS-chuh-rized) - something that has not been pasteurized. Pasteurization is the process of heating a substance, especially a liquid, for a certain amount of time. This process destroys bacteria or other harmful organisms without otherwise changing the substance.

To learn more about avoiding hidden dangers, visit ABDO Publishing Company online. Web sites about food safety are featured on our Book Links page. These links are routinely monitored and updated to provide the most current information available.
www.abdopublishing.com

Index